Entertainment

NEW YORK
SHOPPING
GUIDE 2020

RECOMMENDED STORES FOR VISITORS

The Most Positively
Reviewed and Recommended
Stores in the City

EGP
Editorial

NEW YORK SHOPPING GUIDE 2020
Best Rated Stores in New York, NY

© Stephanie S. McNaught, 2020
© E.G.P. Editorial, 2020

Printed in USA.

ISBN-13: 9781080022199

NEW YORK SHOPPING GUIDE 2020

Most Recommended Stores in New York

This directory is dedicated to New York Business Owners and Managers
who provide the experience that the locals and tourists enjoy.
Thanks you very much for all that you do and thank for being the "People Choice".

Thanks to everyone that posts their reviews online and
the amazing reviews sites that make our life easier.

The places listed in this book are the most positively reviewed
and recommended by locals and travelers from around the world.

Thank you for your time and enjoy the directory that is
designed with locals and tourist in mind!

TOP 500
SHOPPING SPOTS

The Most Recommended
(from #1 to #500)

#1
Meg
Category: Women's Clothing
Average Price: Modest
Area: East Village
Address: 312 E 9th St
New York, NY 10003
Phone: (212) 260-6329

#2
Fuego 718
Category: Home Decor, Arts, Crafts
Average Price: Modest
Area: Williamsburg - South Side,
Williamsburg - North Side
Address: 249 Grand St
Brooklyn, NY 11211
Phone: (718) 302-2913

#3
The Market NYC
Category: Women's Clothing,
Men's Clothing, Jewelry
Average Price: Modest
Area: Greenwich Village
Address: 159 Bleecker Street
New York, NY 10012
Phone: (646) 691-4525

#4
Rosebud Vintage
At The Peacock Room
Category: Used, Vintage
Average Price: Modest
Area: Crown Heights
Address: 721 Franklin Ave
Brooklyn, NY 11238
Phone: (347) 435-0568

#5
Urban Jungle
Category: Used, Vintage, Thrift Store
Average Price: Inexpensive
Area: East Williamsburg, Bushwick
Address: 118 Knickerbocker St
Brooklyn, NY 11237
Phone: (718) 381-8510

#6
Catland
Category: Bookstore,
Average Price: Modest
Area: East Williamsburg, Bushwick
Address: 987 Flushing Ave
Brooklyn, NY 11206
Phone: (718) 418-9393

#7
Uniqlo
Category: Women's Clothing,
Men's Clothing, Children's Clothing
Average Price: Modest
Area: Midtown West
Address: 31 W 34th St
New York, NY 10001
Phone: (877) 486-4756

#8
Kamakura Shirts
Category: Men's Clothing,
Women's Clothing, Formal Wear
Average Price: Modest
Area: Midtown East
Address: 400 Madison Ave
New York, NY 10017
Phone: (212) 308-5266

#9
Article&
Category: Women's Clothing, Accessories
Average Price: Expensive
Area: Cobble Hill, Gowanus
Address: 198 Smith St
Brooklyn, NY 11231
Phone: (718) 852-3620

#10
Swallow
Category: Gift Shop
Average Price: Expensive
Area: Carroll Gardens, Gowanus
Address: 361 Smith St
Brooklyn, NY 11231
Phone: (718) 222-8201

#11
Lockwood
Category: Women's Clothing,
Home Decor, Accessories
Average Price: Modest
Area: Astoria
Address: 3215 33rd St
Astoria, NY 11106
Phone: (718) 626-6030

#12
Brooklyn Superhero Supply Co
Category: Toy Store,
Average Price: Modest
Area: Park Slope
Address: 372 5th Ave
Brooklyn, NY 11215
Phone: (718) 499-9884

#13
Treehouse Brooklyn
Category: Women's Clothing
Average Price: Modest
Area: East Williamsburg
Address: 430 Graham Ave
Brooklyn, NY 11226
Phone: (718) 482-8733

#14
My Plastic Heart
Category: Toy Store
Average Price: Modest
Area: Lower East Side
Address: 210 Forsyth St
New York, NY 10002
Phone: (646) 290-6866

#15
Auh2o
Category: Used, Vintage,
Antiques, Thrift Store
Average Price: Inexpensive
Area: East Village
Address: 84 E 7th St
New York, NY 10003
Phone: (212) 466-0844

#16
Brooklyn Denim Co
Category: Accessories, Men's Clothing,
Women's Clothing
Average Price: Expensive
Area: Williamsburg - North Side
Address: 85 N 3rd St
Brooklyn, NY 11249
Phone: (718) 782-2600

#17
Cloak & Dagger
Category: Women's Clothing,
Jewelry, Accessories
Average Price: Expensive
Area: East Village, Alphabet City
Address: 441 E 9th St
New York, NY 10009
Phone: (212) 673-0500

#18
Uniqlo
Category: Women's Clothing,
Men's Clothing, Children's Clothing
Average Price: Modest
Area: Soho
Address: 546 Broadway
New York, NY 10012
Phone: (877) 486-4756

#19
Blue In Green
Category: Men's Clothing
Average Price: Expensive
Area: Soho, Tribeca
Address: 8 Greene St
New York, NY 10013
Phone: (212) 680-0555

#20
Bash & Bow
Category: Gift Shop, Jewelry,
Women's Clothing
Average Price: Modest
Area: Gramercy
Address: 210 E 21st St
New York, NY 10010
Phone: (646) 494-9412

#21
Nordstrom Rack
Category: Department Store
Average Price: Modest
Area: Greenwich Village, Union Square,
Gramercy, Flatiron, East Village
Address: 60 E 14th St
New York, NY 10003
Phone: (212) 220-2080

#22
Ridgewood Market
Category: Flea Market, Arts, Crafts,
Used, Vintage
Average Price: Modest
Area: Ridgewood
Address: 657 Fairview Ave
Ridgewood, NY 11385
Phone: (347) 460-7549

#23
Uniqlo
Category: Women's Clothing,
Men's Clothing, Children's Clothing
Average Price: Modest
Area: Midtown West
Address: 666 5th Ave
New York, NY 10103
Phone: (877) 486-4756

#24
Random Accessories
Category: Jewelry, Cards, Stationery,
Baby Gear, Furniture
Average Price: Modest
Area: East Village
Address: 77 E 4th St
New York, NY 10003
Phone: (212) 358-0650

#25
M.A.E. Vintage And Luxury Consignment
Category: Used, Vintage
Average Price: Modest
Area: South Slope
Address: 461 7th Ave
Brooklyn, NY 11215
Phone: (718) 788-7070

#26
Erie Basin
Category: Jewelry, Antiques
Average Price: Modest
Area: Red Hook
Address: 388 Van Brunt St
Brooklyn, NY 11231
Phone: (718) 554-6147

#27
Rena Reborn
Category: Thrift Store
Average Price: Inexpensive
Area: East Village, Alphabet City
Address: 117 E 7th St
New York, NY 10009
Phone: (212) 253-2595

#28
Oo35mm
Category: Toy Store, Cosmetics, Beauty Supply, Gift Shop
Average Price: Modest
Area: Chinatown
Address: 81 Mott St
New York, NY 10013
Phone: (718) 496-8163

#29
Owl & Thistle General Store
Category: Gift Shop, Home Decor
Average Price: Modest
Area: Crown Heights
Address: 833 Franklin Ave
New York, NY 11225
Phone: (347) 722-5836

#30
No Relation Vintage
Category: Used, Vintage, Thrift Store
Average Price: Inexpensive
Area: East Village
Address: 204 1st Ave
New York, NY 10009
Phone: (212) 228-5201

#31
Tatyana Boutique
Category: Women's Clothing, Accessories
Average Price: Modest
Area: East Village, Noho
Address: 303 Bowery St
New York, NY 10003
Phone: (646) 478-7006

#33
Alter
Category: Men's Clothing, Accessories
Average Price: Modest
Area: Greenpoint
Address: 109 Franklin St
Brooklyn, NY 11222
Phone: (718) 784-8811

#32
Milly & Earl
Category: Accessories, Jewelry
Average Price: Modest
Area: Williamsburg - North Side
Address: 351 Graham Ave
Brooklyn, NY 11211
Phone: (718) 389-0901

#34
Moma Design Store Soho
Category: Home Decor, Watches
Average Price: Expensive
Area: Soho
Address: 81 Spring St
New York, NY 10012
Phone: (646) 613-1367

#35
The Brass Owl
Category: Shoe Store, Jewelry, Accessories
Average Price: Modest
Area: Astoria
Address: 36-19 Ditmars Blvd
Astoria, NY 11105
Phone: (347) 848-0905

#36
Century 21
Category: Department Store
Average Price: Modest
Area: Financial District
Address: 22 Cortlandt St
New York, NY 10007
Phone: (212) 227-9092

#37
BookBook
Category: Bookstore
Average Price: Inexpensive
Area: West Village
Address: 266 Bleecker St
New York, NY 10014
Phone: (212) 807-0180

#38
Stray Vintage
Category: Used, Vintage
Average Price: Modest
Area: Woodside
Address: 4809 Skillman Ave
Sunnyside, NY 11104
Phone: (718) 779-7795

#39
Bloomingdale's Soho
Category: Department Store
Average Price: Expensive
Area: Soho
Address: 504 Broadway
New York, NY 10012
Phone: (212) 729-5900

#40
Rockefeller Center
Category: Landmark/Historical, Shopping
Center
Average Price: Modest
Area: Midtown West
Address: 30 Rockefeller Plz
New York, NY 10012
Phone: (212) 632-3975

#41
Line & Label
Category: Women's Clothing,
Leather Goods, Jewelry
Average Price: Modest
Area: Greenpoint
Address: 568 Manhattan Ave
Brooklyn, NY 11222
Phone: (347) 384-2678

#42
Reformation
Category: Women's Clothing
Average Price: Modest
Area: Lower East Side
Address: 156 Ludlow St
New York, NY 10002
Phone: (646) 448-4925

#43
Babeland
Category: Adult
Average Price: Modest
Area: Lower East Side
Address: 94 Rivington St
New York, NY 10002
Phone: (212) 375-1701

#44
A&J Lingerie And More
Category: Discount Store, Adult
Average Price: Inexpensive
Area: Flatiron
Address: 41 W 28th St
New York, NY 10001
Phone: (212) 779-1141

#45
STORY
Category: Accessories, Men's Clothing,
Women's Clothing
Average Price: Modest
Area: Chelsea
Address: 144 10th Ave
New York, NY 10011
Phone: (212) 242-4853

#46
WORD
Category: Bookstore
Average Price: Modest
Area: Greenpoint
Address: 126 Franklin St
Brooklyn, NY 11222
Phone: (718) 383-0096

#47
Yaf Sparkle
Category: Jewelry, Leather Goods,
Accessories
Average Price: Modest
Area: Lower East Side
Address: 158 Orchard St
New York, NY 10002
Phone: (212) 254-0460

#48
Toy Tokyo
Category: Toy Store
Average Price: Modest
Area: East Village
Address: 91 2nd Ave
New York, NY 10003
Phone: (212) 673-5424

#49
Bra Tenders
Category: Women's Clothing, Department Store
Average Price: Expensive
Area: Hell's Kitchen, Midtown West, Theater District
Address: 630 9th Ave
New York, NY 10036
Phone: (212) 957-7000

#50
Housing Works Thrift Shop
Category: Used, Vintage, Thrift Store
Average Price: Modest
Area: West Village
Address: 245 W 10th St
New York, NY 10014
Phone: (212) 352-1618

#51
Sustainable NYC
Category: Department Store
Average Price: Modest
Area: East Village, Alphabet City
Address: 139 Avenue A
New York, NY 10009
Phone: (212) 254-5400

#52
Pippin Vintage Jewelry
Category: Jewelry, Antiques
Average Price: Modest
Area: Chelsea
Address: 112 W 17th St
New York, NY 10011
Phone: (212) 505-5159

#53
In God We Trust
Category: Women's Clothing, Jewelry, Men's Clothing
Average Price: Expensive
Area: Soho, Nolita
Address: 265 Lafayette St
New York, NY 10012
Phone: (212) 966-9010

#54
Brooklyn Charm
Category: Jewelry, Accessories
Average Price: Modest
Area: Williamsburg - North Side
Address: 145 Bedford Ave
Brooklyn, NY 11211
Phone: (347) 689-2492

#55
Forever 21
Category: Women's Clothing, Men's Clothing
Average Price: Inexpensive
Area: Midtown West, Theater District
Address: 1540 Broadway
New York, NY 10036
Phone: (212) 302-0594

#56
Brookfield Place
Category: Shopping Center
Average Price: Expensive
Area: Financial District, Battery Park
Address: 220 Vesey St
New York, NY 10281
Phone: (212) 417-7000

#57
Miss Master's Closet
Category: Used, Vintage, Arts, Crafts
Average Price: Modest
Area: Bedford Stuyvesant
Address: 1070 Bedford Ave
Brooklyn, NY 11216
Phone: (718) 783-2979

#58
Brooklyn General
Category: Fabric Store, Hobby Shop
Average Price: Modest
Area: Carroll Gardens, Columbia Street Waterfront District
Address: 128 Union St
Brooklyn, NY 11231
Phone: (718) 237-7753

#59
Army & Navy Bags
Category: Luggage, Men's Clothing, Hobby Shop
Average Price: Inexpensive
Area: Lower East Side
Address: 177 E Houston St
New York, NY 10002
Phone: (212) 228-5267

#60
Film Biz Recycling
Category: Thrift Store, Art Supplies, Furniture Store
Average Price: Inexpensive
Area: Gowanus
Address: 540 President St
Brooklyn, NY 11215
Phone: (347) 384-2336

#61
Lot Less Closeouts
Category: Discount Store
Average Price: Inexpensive
Area: Financial District
Address: 95 Fulton St
New York, NY 10038
Phone: (212) 566-8504

#62
The Evolution Store
Category: Home Decor, Hobby Shop
Average Price: Expensive
Area: Soho
Address: 120 Spring St
New York, NY 10012
Phone: (212) 343-1114

#63
Green In BKLYN
Category: Department Store, Gift Shop
Average Price: Modest
Area: Clinton Hill
Address: 432 Myrtle Ave
Brooklyn, NY 11205
Phone: (718) 855-4383

#64
The Little Lebowski Shop
Category: Books, Mags, Music,
Video, Hobby Shop
Average Price: Modest
Area: Greenwich Village
Address: 215 Thompson St
New York, NY 10012
Phone: (212) 388-1466

#65
Pops Popular Clothing
Category: Men's Clothing
Average Price: Modest
Area: Greenpoint
Address: 7 Franklin St
Brooklyn, NY 11222
Phone: (718) 349-7677

#66
In God We Trust
Category: Jewelry, Women's Clothing,
Men's Clothing
Average Price: Expensive
Area: Greenpoint
Address: 70 Greenpoint Ave
Brooklyn, NY 11222
Phone: (718) 389-3545

#67
Babeland
Category: Adult
Average Price: Modest
Area: Soho
Address: 43 Mercer St
New York, NY 10013
Phone: (212) 966-2120

#68
Flushing Mall
Category: Shopping Center,
Food Stand, Caterer
Average Price: Inexpensive
Area: Downtown Flushing, Flushing
Address: 133-31 39th Ave
Flushing, NY 11354
Phone: (718) 886-5814

#69
7115 By Szeki
Category: Women's Clothing, Jewelry
Average Price: Modest
Area: Lower East Side
Address: 157 Rivington St
New York, NY 10002
Phone: (212) 614-3138

#70
Slapback
Category: Women's Clothing
Average Price: Modest
Area: Williamsburg - North Side
Address: 490 Metropolitan Ave
Brooklyn, NY 11211
Phone: (347) 227-7133

#71
Hooti Couture
Category: Thrift Store, Accessories,
Used, Vintage
Average Price: Modest
Area: Prospect Heights
Address: 321 Flatbush Ave
Brooklyn, NY 11217
Phone: (718) 857-1977

#72
Urban Outfitters
Category: Men's Clothing, Women's Clothing
Average Price: Expensive
Area: East Village
Address: 162 2nd Ave
New York, NY 10003
Phone: (212) 375-1277

#73
Fanaberie
Category: Women's Clothing
Average Price: Modest
Area: Greenpoint
Address: 102A Nassau Ave
Brooklyn, NY 11222
Phone: (347) 987-3929

#74
Cure Thrift Shop
Category: Antiques, Thrift Store
Average Price: Modest
Area: East Village
Address: 111 E 12th St
New York, NY 10003
Phone: (212) 505-7467

#75
The Mysterious Bookshop
Category: Bookstore
Average Price: Modest
Area: Tribeca
Address: 58 Warren St
New York, NY 10007
Phone: (212) 587-1011

#76
Housing Works Thrift Shop
Category: Used, Vintage, Thrift Store
Average Price: Inexpensive
Area: Upper West Side
Address: 306 Columbus Ave
New York, NY 10023
Phone: (212) 579-7566

#77
Cadillac's Castle
Category: Used, Vintage,
Women's Clothing, Accessories
Average Price: Modest
Area: East Village
Address: 333 E 9th St
New York, NY 10003
Phone: (212) 475-0406

#78
Vintage Thrift Shop
Category: Used, Vintage, Thrift Store
Average Price: Modest
Area: Gramercy
Address: 286 3rd Ave
New York, NY 10010
Phone: (212) 871-0777

#79
Self Edge
Category: Men's Clothing
Average Price: Expensive
Area: Lower East Side
Address: 157 Orchard St
New York, NY 10002
Phone: (212) 388-0079

#80
Madewell
Category: Women's Clothing, Accessories
Average Price: Modest
Area: Soho
Address: 486 Broadway
New York, NY 10013
Phone: (212) 226-6954

#81
**Unoppressive Non-Imperialist
Bargain Books**
Category: Bookstore
Average Price: Inexpensive
Area: West Village
Address: 34 Carmine St
New York, NY 10014
Phone: (212) 229-0079

#82
H&M
Category: Men's Clothing, Women's Clothing
Average Price: Modest
Area: Midtown West, Midtown East
Address: 640 5th Ave
New York, NY 10019
Phone: (212) 489-0390

#83
The Pleasure Chest
Category: Adult
Average Price: Modest
Area: Upper East Side
Address: 1150 2nd Ave
New York, NY 10065
Phone: (212) 355-6909

#84
LIC Flea & Food
Category: Flea Market, Specialty Food
Average Price: Modest
Area: Hunters Point, Long Island City
Address: 5-25 46th Ave
Long Island City, NY 11101
Phone: (718) 866-8089

#85
Purdy Girl
Category: Women's Clothing
Average Price: Modest
Area: Greenwich Village
Address: 540 Lagaurdia Pl
New York, NY 10012
Phone: (646) 654-6751

#86
Fine And Dandy
Category: Accessories, Men's Clothing, Hats
Average Price: Modest
Area: Hell's Kitchen, Midtown West
Address: 445 W 49th St
New York, NY 10019
Phone: (212) 247-4847

#87
LIC: Living
Category: Women's Clothing,
Home Decor, Jewelry
Average Price: Modest
Area: Hunters Point, Long Island City
Address: 535 51st Ave
Long Island City, NY 11101
Phone: (718) 361-5650

#88
Saffron Brooklyn
Category: Flowers, Gifts
Average Price: Modest
Area: Fort Greene
Address: 31 Hanson Pl
Brooklyn, NY 11217
Phone: (718) 852-6053

#89
Victors Villa Furniture
Category: Furniture Store
Average Price: Modest
Area: Astoria
Address: 3209 Broadway
Queens, NY 11106
Phone: (718) 545-0244

#90
Foxy & Winston
Category: Cards, Stationery,
Home Decor, Gift Shop
Average Price: Modest
Area: Red Hook
Address: 392 Van Brunt St
Brooklyn, NY 11231
Phone: (718) 928-4855

#91
Anthropologie
Category: Women's Clothing, Home Decor
Average Price: Expensive
Area: Soho
Address: 375 W Broadway
New York, NY 10012
Phone: (212) 343-7070

#92
The Dressing Room
Category: Bar, Used, Vintage
Average Price: Modest
Area: Lower East Side
Address: 75A Orchard St
New York, NY 10002
Phone: (212) 966-7330

#93
Miomia
Category: Skin Care, Cosmetics,
Beauty Supply
Average Price: Expensive
Area: Williamsburg - South Side
Address: 318 Bedford Ave
Brooklyn, NY 11211
Phone: (718) 490-5599

#94
Star Struck Vintage Clothing
Category: Used, Vintage
Average Price: Modest
Area: West Village
Address: 47 Greenwich Ave
New York, NY 10014
Phone: (212) 691-5357

#95
Amazing Savings Of Brooklyn
Category: Department Store
Average Price: Inexpensive
Area: Borough Park
Address: 1080 Mcdonald Ave
Brooklyn, NY 11230
Phone: (718) 253-2244

#96
Sunnyside Thrift Shop
Category: Thrift Store
Average Price: Inexpensive
Area: Sunnyside
Address: 45-14 Greenpoint Ave
Sunnyside, NY 11104
Phone: (718) 786-7780

#97
Union Square Holiday Market
Category: Shopping Center
Average Price: Modest
Area: Union Square, Flatiron, East Village
Address: Union Sq & W 14th St
New York, NY 10003
Phone: (212) 529-9262

#98
Closetdash
Category: Women's Clothing, Used, Vintage
Average Price: Modest
Area: Sunnyside
Address: 45-50 30th St
Long Island City, NY 11101
Phone: (800) 230-4590

#99
FAO Schwarz
Category: Toy Store
Average Price: Expensive
Area: Midtown East
Address: 767 5th Ave
New York, NY 10153
Phone: (212) 644-9400

#100
Color BKLYN
Category: Gift Shop
Average Price: Modest
Area: Prospect Heights
Address: 760 Washington Ave
Brooklyn, NY 11238
Phone: (718) 399-3631

#101
Cloth
Category: Women's Clothing
Average Price: Modest
Area: Fort Greene
Address: 138 Fort Greene Place
Brooklyn, NY 11217
Phone: (718) 403-0223

#102
Fishs Eddy
Category: Kitchen & Bath
Average Price: Modest
Area: Flatiron
Address: 889 Broadway
New York, NY 10003
Phone: (212) 420-9020

#103
Prive Designer Sales
Category: Women's Clothing, Men's Clothing
Average Price: Modest
Area: Chelsea, Meatpacking District
Address: 75 9th Ave
New York, NY 10011
Phone: (212) 543-4300

#104
APC
Category: Men's Clothing, Women's Clothing
Average Price: Expensive
Area: Soho
Address: 131 Mercer St
New York, NY 10012
Phone: (212) 966-9685

#105
Stick, Stone & Bone
Category: Hobby Shop
Average Price: Modest
Area: West Village
Address: 111 Christopher St
New York, NY 10014
Phone: (212) 807-7024

#106
By Brooklyn
Category: Local Flavor, Cards,
Stationery, Gift Shop
Average Price: Modest
Area: Cobble Hill, Gowanus
Address: 261 Smith St
Brooklyn, NY 11231
Phone: (718) 643-0606

#107
Saks Fifth Avenue
Category: Department Store
Average Price: Exclusive
Area: Midtown East
Address: 611 5th Ave
New York, NY 10022
Phone: (212) 753-4000

#108
Proper Cloth
Category: Men's Clothing
Average Price: Expensive
Area: Soho
Address: 450 Broadway
New York, NY 10013
Phone: (646) 964-4221

#109
Koryo Bookstore
Category: Bookstore
Average Price: Modest
Area: Midtown West, Koreatown
Address: 35 W 32nd St
New York, NY 10001
Phone: (212) 564-1844

#110
The Compleat Strategist
Category: Hobby Shop
Average Price: Expensive
Area: Midtown East
Address: 11 E 33rd St
New York, NY 10016
Phone: (212) 685-3880

#111
Muji
Category: Women's Clothing,
Accessories, Department Store
Average Price: Modest
Area: Midtown West, Theater District
Address: 620 8th Ave
New York, NY 10018
Phone: (212) 382-2300

#112
Scent Elate
Category: Home Decor
Average Price: Modest
Area: Hell's Kitchen, Midtown West,
Theater District
Address: 313 W 48th St
New York, NY 10036
Phone: (212) 258-3043

#113
Olly Oxen Free Vintage
Category: Thrift Store, Used, Vintage
Average Price: Modest
Area: East Williamsburg
Address: 137 Montrose Ave
Brooklyn, NY 11206
Phone: (347) 860-3406

#114
Kadonyc
Category: Gift Shop, Cards,
Stationery, Home Decor
Average Price: Expensive
Area: Greenwich Village
Address: 192 Bleecker St
New York, NY 10012
Phone: (917) 793-5400

#115
The One Well
Category: Jewelry, Home Decor, Accessories
Average Price: Modest
Area: Greenpoint
Address: 165 Greenpoint Ave
Brooklyn, NY 11222
Phone: (347) 889-6792

#116
Pearl River Mart
Category: Department Store, Home Decor
Average Price: Modest
Area: Soho
Address: 477 Broadway
New York, NY 10013
Phone: (800) 878-2446

#117
Christian Louboutin
Category: Shoe Store
Average Price: Exclusive
Area: Midtown East
Address: 965 Madison Ave
New York, NY 10022
Phone: (212) 396-1884

#118
Loren
Category: Women's Clothing,
Men's Clothing, Used, Vintage
Average Price: Modest
Area: Greenpoint
Address: 80 Nassau Ave
Brooklyn, NY 11222
Phone: (347) 529-5771

#119
Dolly G's
Category: Used, Vintage, Women's Clothing
Average Price: Modest
Area: East Williamsburg
Address: 320 Graham Ave
Brooklyn, NY 11211
Phone: (718) 599-1044

#120
Darling
Category: Women's Clothing,
Accessories, Bridal
Average Price: Modest
Area: West Village
Address: 1 Horatio St
New York, NY 10014
Phone: (646) 336-6966

#121
Net-A-Porter.Com
Category: Fashion
Average Price: Exclusive
Area: Hunters Point, Long Island City
Address: 30-30 47th Ave
Long Island City, NY 11101
Phone: (800) 481-1064

#122
Century 21
Category: Department Store
Average Price: Modest
Area: Bay Ridge
Address: 472 86th St
Brooklyn, NY 11209
Phone: (718) 748-3266

#123
Awoke Vintage
Category: Used, Vintage
Average Price: Modest
Area: Williamsburg - North Side
Address: 132 N5th St
Brooklyn, NY 11211
Phone: (718) 387-3130

#124
Club Monaco
Category: Sports Wear, Men's Clothing,
Women's Clothing
Average Price: Expensive
Area: Flatiron
Address: 160 5th Ave
New York, NY 10010
Phone: (212) 352-0936

#125
Stella Dallas
Category: Used, Vintage
Average Price: Modest
Area: Greenwich Village
Address: 218 Thompson St
New York, NY 10012
Phone: (212) 674-0447

#126
Muji
Category: Department Store
Average Price: Modest
Area: Flatiron
Address: 16 W 19th St
New York, NY 10011
Phone: (212) 414-9024

#127
Jack's
Category: Discount Store
Average Price: Inexpensive
Area: Midtown West
Address: 110 W 32nd St
New York, NY 10001
Phone: (212) 268-9962

#128
Anthropologie
Category: Women's Clothing, Home Decor
Average Price: Expensive
Area: Midtown West
Address: 50 Rockefeller Plz
New York, NY 10020
Phone: (212) 246-0386

#129
DSW Designer Shoe Warehouse
Category: Shoe Store
Average Price: Modest
Area: Midtown West
Address: 213 West 34th Street
New York, NY 10001
Phone: (212) 967-9703

#130
Elizabeth Center Gift Shops
Category: Arts, Crafts
Average Price: Inexpensive
Area: Chinatown
Address: 15 Elizabeth St
New York, NY 10013
Phone: (212) 431-5150

#131
Jeremy Argyle NYC
Category: Men's Clothing
Average Price: Expensive
Area: Soho
Address: 160 Spring St
New York, NY 10012
Phone: (646) 781-9050

#132
Goorin Bros.
Category: Accessories, Hats
Average Price: Modest
Area: Park Slope
Address: 195 5th Avenue
Brooklyn, NY 11217
Phone: (718) 783-4287

#133
Lot Less Closeouts
Category: Department Store
Average Price: Inexpensive
Area: Civic Center, Tribeca
Address: 97 Chambers St
New York, NY 10007
Phone: (212) 233-0607

#134
NOS Boutique
Category: Shoe Store, Men's Clothing,
Women's Clothing
Average Price: Expensive
Area: DUMBO
Address: 81 Front St
Brooklyn, NY 11201
Phone: (718) 422-0095

#135
Old Hollywood
Category: Jewelry, Accessories,
Women's Clothing
Average Price: Modest
Area: Greenpoint
Address: 99 Franklin St
Brooklyn, NY 11222
Phone: (718) 389-0837

#136
Bergdorf Goodman
Category: Women's Clothing,
Men's Clothing, Children's Clothing
Average Price: Exclusive
Area: Midtown West
Address: 754 5th Ave
New York, NY 10019
Phone: (800) 558-1855

#137
Better Than Jam
Category: Women's Clothing,
Jewelry, Arts, Crafts
Average Price: Modest
Area: East Williamsburg, Bushwick
Address: 123 Knickerbocker Ave
Brooklyn, NY 11237
Phone: (631) 377-2500

#138
Jane's Closet
Category: Women's Clothing
Average Price: Modest
Area: Williamsburg - North Side
Address: 60 N 6th St
Brooklyn, NY 11249
Phone: (718) 384-0437

#139
Birchbox Soho
Category: Cosmetics, Beauty Supply
Average Price: Modest
Area: Soho
Address: 433 W Broadway
New York, NY 10012
Phone: (646) 589-8500

#140
Jillery
Category: Jewelry, Used, Vintage
Average Price: Modest
Area: East Village, Alphabet City
Address: 107 Ave B
New York, NY 10009
Phone: (212) 674-9383

#141
TJ Maxx
Category: Department Store
Average Price: Modest
Area: Financial District
Address: 14 Wall St
New York, NY 10005
Phone: (212) 587-8459

#142
Homebody Boutique
Category: Jewelry, Cards,
Stationery, Gift Shop
Average Price: Modest
Area: South Slope
Address: 449 7th Ave
Brooklyn, NY 11215
Phone: (718) 369-8980

#143
Onassis Clothing
Category: Men's Clothing
Average Price: Modest
Area: Soho
Address: 71 Greene St
New York, NY 10012
Phone: (212) 966-8869

#144
Babeland
Category: Adult
Average Price: Modest
Area: Park Slope
Address: 462 Bergen St
Brooklyn, NY 11217
Phone: (718) 638-3820

#145
Macy's
Category: Department Store, Men's Clothing, Women's Clothing
Average Price: Modest
Area: Midtown West
Address: 151 W 34th St
New York, NY 10001
Phone: (212) 695-4400

#146
Urban Alchemist
Category: Fashion, Jewelry
Average Price: Modest
Area: Park Slope
Address: 343 5th St
Brooklyn, NY 11215
Phone: (718) 499-0758

#147
Mystique Boutique
Category: Women's Clothing
Average Price: Inexpensive
Area: Soho
Address: 547 Broadway
New York, NY 10012
Phone: (212) 274-0645

#148
Pork Pie Hatters
Category: Accessories
Average Price: Modest
Area: East Village, Alphabet City
Address: 440 E 9th St
Manhattan, NY 10009
Phone: (212) 260-0408

#149
Mooshoes
Category: Shoe Store
Average Price: Expensive
Area: Lower East Side
Address: 78 Orchard St
New York, NY 10002
Phone: (212) 254-6512

#150
Dave's New York
Category: Shoe Store, Men's Clothing
Average Price: Modest
Area: Flatiron
Address: 581 Ave Of The Americas
New York, NY 10011
Phone: (212) 989-6444

#151
Land Of Buddha
Category: Antiques, Home Decor
Average Price: Modest
Area: Greenwich Village
Address: 128 Macdougal St
New York, NY 10012
Phone: (646) 602-6588

#152
Authentiques
Category: Antiques
Average Price: Modest
Area: Chelsea
Address: 255 W 18th St
New York, NY 10011
Phone: (212) 675-2179

#153
Flirt
Category: Women's Clothing
Average Price: Expensive
Area: Park Slope
Address: 93 5th Ave
Brooklyn, NY 11217
Phone: (718) 783-0364

#154
Yesterday's News
Category: Antiques
Average Price: Inexpensive
Area: Carroll Gardens
Address: 428 Court St
Brooklyn, NY 11231
Phone: (718) 875-0546

#155
Forbidden Planet
Category: Toy Store, Comic Books
Average Price: Modest
Area: Greenwich Village, Union Square, East Village
Address: 832 Broadway
New York, NY 10003
Phone: (212) 473-1576

#156
Whisk
Category: Kitchen & Bath
Average Price: Modest
Area: Williamsburg - North Side
Address: 231 Bedford Ave
Brooklyn, NY 11211
Phone: (718) 218-7230

#157
Free People
Category: Accessories, Shoe Store,
Women's Clothing
Average Price: Expensive
Area: Cobble Hill, Boerum Hill
Address: 113 Smith St
Brooklyn, NY 11201
Phone: (718) 250-0050

#158
Little Shop Of Crafts
Category: Arts, Crafts,
Average Price: Modest
Area: Upper West Side
Address: 711 Amsterdam Ave
New York, NY 10025
Phone: (212) 531-2723

#159
John Derian
Category: Home Decor
Average Price: Exclusive
Area: East Village
Address: 6 E 2nd St
New York, NY 10003
Phone: (212) 677-3917

#160
Yumi Kim
Category: Women's Clothing
Average Price: Modest
Area: Lower East Side
Address: 105 Stanton St
New York, NY 10002
Phone: (212) 420-5919

#161
Greenflea Market
Category: Antiques, Used, Vintage,
Farmers Market
Average Price: Modest
Area: Upper West Side
Address: 100 W 77th St
New York, NY 10024
Phone: (212) 239-3025

#162
Kinokuniya Bookstores
Category: Bookstore, Cards, Stationery
Average Price: Modest
Area: Midtown West, Theater District
Address: 1073 Ave Of The Americas
New York, NY 10018
Phone: (212) 869-1700

#163
Unnameable Books
Category: Bookstore
Average Price: Modest
Area: Prospect Heights
Address: 600 Vanderbilt Ave
Brooklyn, NY 11238
Phone: (718) 789-1534

#164
Underground Thrift Store
Category: Thrift Store
Average Price: Inexpensive
Area: Brooklyn Heights
Address: 75 Hicks St
Brooklyn, NY 11201
Phone: (718) 624-4743

#165
Clementine Consignment
Category: Used, Vintage, Maternity Wear
Average Price: Inexpensive
Area: Greenwich Village
Address: 39 1/2 Washington Sq S
New York, NY 10012
Phone: (212) 228-9333

#166
Free People Clothing Boutique
Category: Fashion
Average Price: Expensive
Area: Union Square, Flatiron
Address: 79 5th Ave
New York, NY 10003
Phone: (212) 647-1293

#167
Christian Louboutin
Category: Shoe Store
Average Price: Exclusive
Area: West Village
Address: 59 Horatio St
New York, NY 10184
Phone: (212) 255-1910

#168
Rue St Denis Clothier Ltd
Category: Used, Vintage
Average Price: Modest
Area: East Village, Alphabet City
Address: 170 Ave B
New York, NY 10009
Phone: (212) 260-3388

#169
Kiteya Soho
Category: Accessories, Cards,
Stationery, Home Decor
Average Price: Modest
Area: Soho
Address: 464 Broome St
New York, NY 10013
Phone: (212) 219-7505

#170
Human Head Records
Category: Vinyl Records
Average Price: Inexpensive
Area: East Williamsburg
Address: 168 Johnson Ave
Brooklyn, NY 11206
Phone: (347) 987-3362

#171
Brooklyn Royalty
Category: Fashion
Average Price: Modest
Area: Williamsburg - North Side
Address: 153 Roebling St
Brooklyn, NY 11211
Phone: (917) 349-9155

#172
Costco
Category: Wholesale Store, Tires
Average Price: Modest
Area: Astoria
Address: 32-50 Vernon Blvd
Astoria, NY 11106
Phone: (718) 267-3680

#173
Nasty Pig
Category: Men's Clothing
Average Price: Expensive
Area: Chelsea
Address: 259 West 19th St
New York, NY 10011
Phone: (212) 691-6067

#174
Housing Works Thrift Shop
Category: Used, Vintage, Thrift Store
Average Price: Modest
Area: Chelsea
Address: 143 W 17th St
New York, NY 10011
Phone: (718) 838-5050

#175
Cool Pony
Category: Thrift Store
Average Price: Modest
Area: Crown Heights
Address: 733 Franklin Ave
Brooklyn, NY 11238
Phone: (347) 927-4718

#176
SRG Fashion
Category: Bespoke Clothing, Men's Clothing
Average Price: Inexpensive
Area: Steinway
Address: 1971 41st St
Astoria, NY 11105
Phone: (718) 626-9600

#177
Odin
Category: Men's Clothing
Average Price: Expensive
Area: Soho
Address: 199 Lafayette St
New York, NY 10012
Phone: (212) 966-0026

#178
Patagonia
Category: Outdoor Gear
Average Price: Expensive
Area: Soho
Address: 101 Wooster St
New York, NY 10012
Phone: (212) 343-1776

#179
Lola's Boutique
Category: Women's Clothing
Average Price: Modest
Area: Bay Ridge
Address: 8503 3rd Ave
Brooklyn, NY 11209
Phone: (718) 745-4300

#180
H&M
Category: Accessories, Men's Clothing,
Women's Clothing
Average Price: Inexpensive
Area: Midtown East
Address: 731 Lexington Ave
New York, NY 10022
Phone: (212) 935-6781

#181
If Boutique
Category: Men's Clothing, Women's Clothing
Average Price: Exclusive
Area: Soho
Address: 94 Grand St
New York, NY 10013
Phone: (212) 334-4964

#182
Warby Parker
Category: Eyewear, Opticians, Optometrists
Average Price: Modest
Area: Soho
Address: 121 Greene St
New York, NY 10012
Phone: (646) 568-3720

#183
Twenty Sided Store
Category: Hobby Shop
Average Price: Modest
Area: Williamsburg - South Side
Address: 362 Grand St
Brooklyn, NY 11211
Phone: (718) 963-1578

#184
The Brooklyn Kitchen
Category: Kitchen & Bath, Cooking School
Average Price: Modest
Area: Williamsburg - North Side
Address: 100 Frost St
Brooklyn, NY 11211
Phone: (718) 389-2982

#185
Beau By Aksel Paris
Category: Bespoke Clothing, Formal Wear
Average Price: Modest
Area: Financial District
Address: 222 Broadway
New York, NY 10013
Phone: (888) 992-5735

#186
Backwoods
Category: Accessories, Jewelry
Average Price: Inexpensive
Area: Hell's Kitchen, Midtown West,
Theater District
Address: 42nd St
New York, NY
Phone: (212) 244-4714

#187
Three Lives & Company
Category: Bookstore
Average Price: Modest
Area: West Village
Address: 154 W 10th St
New York, NY 10014
Phone: (212) 741-2069

#188
Mongo
Category: Home Decor, Jewelry, Antiques
Average Price: Modest
Area: Cobble Hill, Carroll Gardens, Gowanus
Address: 246 Smith St
Brooklyn, NY 11217
Phone: (917) 671-7696

#189
La Di Da Dee
Category: Women's Clothing,
Accessories, Jewelry
Average Price: Modest
Area: Williamsburg - South Side
Address: 160 Havemeyer St
Brooklyn, NY 11211
Phone: (347) 689-9086

#190
The Uncommons
Category: Toy Store, Coffee, Tea, Bar
Average Price: Inexpensive
Area: Greenwich Village
Address: 230 Thompson St
New York, NY 10012
Phone: (646) 543-9215

#191
Pinkyotto
Category: Women's Clothing, Jewelry
Average Price: Expensive
Area: East Village
Address: 307 E 9th St
New York, NY 10003
Phone: (212) 533-4028

#192
Pippin Vintage Home
Category: Antiques
Average Price: Modest
Area: Chelsea
Address: 112 1/2 W 17th St
New York, NY 10011
Phone: (212) 206-0008

#193
Obscura Antiques
Category: Antiques
Average Price: Expensive
Area: East Village, Alphabet City
Address: 207 Ave A
New York, NY 10009
Phone: (212) 505-9251

#194
Strand Bookstore
Category: Bookstore
Average Price: Inexpensive
Area: Greenwich Village, Union Square,
East Village
Address: 828 Broadway
New York, NY 10003
Phone: (212) 473-1452

#195
Red Wing Shoes
Category: Shoe Store
Average Price: Expensive
Area: Sunnyside
Address: 4701 Queens Blvd
Sunnyside, NY 11104
Phone: (718) 392-2242

#196
Pema NY
Category: Women's Clothing, Accessories
Average Price: Modest
Area: Williamsburg - North Side
Address: 225 Bedford Ave
Brooklyn, NY 11211
Phone: (718) 388-8814

#197
Fox & Fawn
Category: Used, Vintage, Thrift Store
Average Price: Modest
Area: Greenpoint
Address: 570 Manhattan Ave
Brooklyn, NY 11222
Phone: (718) 349-9510

#198
Goldy & Mac
Category: Women's Clothing, Accessories
Average Price: Modest
Area: South Slope, Park Slope
Address: 396 7th Ave
Brooklyn, NY 11215
Phone: (718) 832-4868

#199
Village Tannery
Category: Leather Goods
Average Price: Expensive
Area: Greenwich Village
Address: 173 Bleecker St
New York, NY 10012
Phone: (212) 673-5444

#200
Union Garage NYC
Category: Motorcycle Gear
Average Price: Modest
Area: Columbia Street Waterfront District
Address: 103 Union St
Brooklyn, NY 11231
Phone: (718) 594-7093

#201
Buffalo Exchange
Category: Used, Vintage, Men's Clothing,
Women's Clothing
Average Price: Modest
Area: Chelsea
Address: 114 W 26th St
New York, NY 10001
Phone: (212) 675-3535

#202
Hell's Kitchen Flea Market
Category: Antiques, Used, Vintage
Average Price: Modest
Area: Chelsea, Midtown West
Address: 39th St
New York, NY 10011
Phone: (212) 243-5343

#203
Arth
Category: Accessories
Average Price: Modest
Area: Soho
Address: 75 W Houston St
New York, NY 10012
Phone: (212) 539-1431

#204
Lot-Less Closeouts
Category: Discount Store
Average Price: Inexpensive
Area: Midtown West, Theater District
Address: 206 W 40th St
New York, NY 10018
Phone: (212) 704-9856

#205
Brooklyn Industries
Category: Men's Clothing, Women's Clothing
Average Price: Modest
Area: Chelsea
Address: 161 8th Ave
New York, NY 10011
Phone: (212) 206-0477

#206
Deals
Category: Discount Store, Department Store
Average Price: Inexpensive
Area: Astoria
Address: 31-72 31 St
Astoria, NY 11106
Phone: (718) 721-0650

#207
Jack's World
Category: Discount Store
Average Price: Inexpensive
Area: Midtown West
Address: 45 W 45th St
New York, NY 10036
Phone: (212) 354-6888

#208
By Robert James
Category: Men's Clothing
Average Price: Expensive
Area: Lower East Side
Address: 74 Orchard St
New York, NY 10002
Phone: (212) 253-2121

#209
Costco
Category: Wholesale Store
Average Price: Modest
Area: Sunset Park
Address: 976 3rd Ave
Brooklyn, NY 11232
Phone: (718) 965-7603

#210
Annie's Blue Ribbon General Store
Category: Cards, Stationery,
Toy Store, Home Decor
Average Price: Modest
Area: Park Slope
Address: 232 5th Ave
Brooklyn, NY 11215
Phone: (718) 522-9848

#211
Still House
Category: Jewelry, Home Decor
Average Price: Modest
Area: East Village, Alphabet City
Address: 117 E 7th St
Manhattan, NY 10003
Phone: (212) 539-0200

#212
Billy Reid
Category: Men's Clothing, Women's Clothing
Average Price: Expensive
Area: Noho
Address: 54 Bond St
New York, NY 10012
Phone: (212) 598-9355

#213
Calabar Imports
Category: Jewelry, Home Decor.
Women's Clothing
Average Price: Modest
Area: Crown Heights
Address: 708 Franklin Ave
Brooklyn, NY 11238
Phone: (718) 638-4288

#214
Kai D
Category: Men's Clothing
Average Price: Expensive
Area: Williamsburg - South Side
Address: 230 Grand St
Brooklyn, NY 11211
Phone: (347) 765-2204

#215
Jeffrey
Category: Shoe Store, Women's Clothing
Average Price: Exclusive
Area: Chelsea, West Village,
Meatpacking District
Address: 449 W 14th St
New York, NY 10014
Phone: (212) 206-1272

#216
Unique Boutique
Category: Used, Vintage
Average Price: Inexpensive
Area: Astoria
Address: 2588 Steinway St
Astoria, NY 11102
Phone: (718) 204-0310

#217
John Fluevog
Category: Shoe Store
Average Price: Expensive
Area: Nolita
Address: 250 Mulberry St
New York, NY 10012
Phone: (212) 431-4484

#218
Zara
Category: Men's Clothing, Women's Clothing
Average Price: Modest
Area: Union Square, Flatiron
Address: 101 5th Ave
New York, NY 10003
Phone: (212) 741-0555

#219
Bradelis New York
Category: Lingerie
Average Price: Expensive
Area: Flatiron
Address: 66 Madison Ave
New York, NY 10016
Phone: (212) 599-2223

#220
City Vape
Category: Vape Shop
Average Price: Modest
Area: Astoria
Address: 31-88 37th St
Astoria, NY 11103
Phone: (347) 730-4944

#221
Whisk
Category: Home Decor, Kitchen & Bath
Average Price: Modest
Area: Flatiron
Address: 933 Broadway
New York, NY 10010
Phone: (212) 477-8680

#222
J.Crew
Category: Accessories, Men's Clothing,
Women's Clothing
Average Price: Expensive
Area: Union Square, Flatiron
Address: 91 Fifth Avenue
New York, NY 10003
Phone: (212) 255-4848

#223
Loveday 31
Category: Used, Vintage
Average Price: Modest
Area: Astoria
Address: 3306 31st Ave
Astoria, NY 11106
Phone: (718) 728-4057

#224
Repop
Category: Art Gallery, Antiques
Average Price: Modest
Area: Williamsburg - North Side
Address: 143 Roebling St
New York, NY 11211
Phone: (718) 260-8032

#225
Mini Mini Market
Category: Women's Clothing,
Accessories, Jewelry
Average Price: Modest
Area: Williamsburg - North Side
Address: 218 Bedford Ave
Brooklyn, NY 11211
Phone: (718) 302-9337

#226
Soula Shoes
Category: Shoe Store
Average Price: Expensive
Area: Cobble Hill, Boerum Hill
Address: 185 Smith St
Brooklyn, NY 11201
Phone: (718) 834-8423

#227
Century 21 Department Store
Category: Department Store
Average Price: Modest
Area: Financial District
Address: 22 Cortlandt St
New York, NY 10007
Phone: (212) 227-9092

#228
Books Of Wonder
Category: Bookstore
Average Price: Modest
Area: Flatiron
Address: 18 W 18th St
New York, NY 10011
Phone: (212) 989-3270

#229
St. Luke's Thrift Shop
Category: Thrift Store
Average Price: Inexpensive
Area: West Village
Address: 487 Hudson St
New York, NY 10014
Phone: (212) 924-9364

#230
Muji
Category: Home Decor, Furniture Store
Average Price: Modest
Area: Soho
Address: 455 Broadway
New York, NY 10013
Phone: (212) 334-2002

#231
TJ Maxx
Category: Department Store
Average Price: Modest
Area: Midtown West
Address: 250 W 57th St
New York, NY 10107
Phone: (212) 245-6201

#232
Target
Category: Department Store
Average Price: Modest
Area: East Harlem
Address: 517 E 117th St
New York, NY 10035
Phone: (212) 835-0860

#233
Acustom Apparel
Category: Men's Clothing
Average Price: Expensive
Area: South Village
Address: 330 W Broadway
New York, NY 10013
Phone: (212) 219-8620

#234
Lingo
Category: Women's Clothing
Average Price: Modest
Area: Chelsea
Address: 257 W 19th St
New York, NY 10011
Phone: (212) 929-4676

#235
Hickoree's Floor Two
Category: Accessories, Men's Clothing
Average Price: Expensive
Area: Williamsburg - South Side, South
Williamsburg
Address: 109 S 6th St
Brooklyn, NY 11211
Phone: (347) 294-0005

#236
Antoinette
Category: Used, Vintage, Accessories
Average Price: Modest
Area: Williamsburg - North Side
Address: 119 Grand St
Brooklyn, NY 11211
Phone: (718) 387-8664

#237
Hung Chong Imports
Category: Kitchen & Bath
Average Price: Inexpensive
Area: Chinatown, Civic Center
Address: 14 Bowery
New York, NY 10013
Phone: (212) 349-3392

#238
TJ Maxx
Category: Department Store
Average Price: Modest
Area: Flatiron
Address: 620 Ave Of The Americas
New York, NY 10011
Phone: (212) 229-0875

#239
Housing Works Bookstore Cafe
Category: Bookstore, Café
Average Price: Inexpensive
Area: Soho
Address: 126 Crosby St
New York, NY 10012
Phone: (212) 334-3324

#240
Flight Club
Category: Shoe Store, Sports Wear
Average Price: Expensive
Area: Greenwich Village, East Village
Address: 812 Broadway
New York, NY 10003
Phone: (888) 937-8020

#241
Love Shine
Category: Accessories, Cards, Stationery
Average Price: Modest
Area: East Village, Alphabet City
Address: 543 E 6th St
New York, NY 10009
Phone: (212) 387-0935

#242
Maison Martin Margiela
Category: Men's Clothing,
Women's Clothing, Leather Goods
Average Price: Exclusive
Area: West Village
Address: 803 Greenwich St
New York, NY 10014
Phone: (212) 989-7612

#243
192 Books
Category: Bookstore
Average Price: Modest
Area: Chelsea
Address: 192 10th Ave
New York, NY 10011
Phone: (212) 255-4022

#244
Deal$
Category: Discount Store
Average Price: Inexpensive
Area: Greenpoint
Address: 680 Meeker Ave
Brooklyn, NY 11222
Phone: (718) 599-2064

#245
Unique
Category: Thrift Store
Average Price: Inexpensive
Area: Downtown Brooklyn
Address: 408 Fulton Street
Brooklyn, NY 11201
Phone: (718) 643-1825

#246
Housing Works Thrift Shop
Category: Antiques, Thrift Store
Average Price: Modest
Area: Tribeca
Address: 119 Chambers St
New York, NY 10007
Phone: (212) 732-0584

#247
Queens Center
Category: Shopping Center
Average Price: Modest
Area: Lefrak City
Address: 9015 Queens Blvd
Elmhurst, NY 11373
Phone: (718) 592-3900

#248
DSW Designer Shoe Warehouse
Category: Shoe Store
Average Price: Modest
Area: Greenwich Village, Union Square
Address: 40 East 14th Street
New York, NY 10003
Phone: (212) 674-2146

#249
Broadway Panhandler
Category: Kitchen & Bath
Average Price: Modest
Area: Greenwich Village
Address: 65 E 8th St
New York, NY 10003
Phone: (212) 966-3434

#250
East Village Thrift Shop
Category: Thrift Store
Average Price: Inexpensive
Area: East Village
Address: 186 2nd Ave
New York, NY 10003
Phone: (212) 375-8585

#251
Patricia Field
Category: Accessories,
Women's Clothing, Costumes
Average Price: Expensive
Area: Noho
Address: 306 Bowery
New York, NY 10012
Phone: (212) 966-4066

#252
Trunk Show Designer Consignment
Category: Personal Shopping, Used, Vintage
Average Price: Exclusive
Area: Harlem
Address: 275-277 W 113th St
New York, NY 10026
Phone: (212) 662-0009

#253
Pink Olive
Category: Children's Clothing,
Cards, Stationery
Average Price: Expensive
Area: East Village, Alphabet City
Address: 439 E 9th St
New York, NY 10009
Phone: (212) 780-0036

#254
Anthropologie
Category: Department Store
Average Price: Expensive
Area: Upper East Side
Address: 1230 3rd Ave
New York, NY 10021
Phone: (800) 309-2500

#255
Barneys New York
Category: Department Store
Average Price: Exclusive
Area: Upper East Side
Address: 660 Madison Ave
New York, NY 10065
Phone: (212) 826-8900

#256
Tiffany & Co
Category: Jewelry
Average Price: Exclusive
Area: Midtown East
Address: 727 5th Ave
New York, NY 10022
Phone: (212) 755-8000

#257
The Henley Vaporium
Category: Vape Shop
Average Price: Modest
Area: Nolita
Address: 23 Cleveland Pl
New York, NY 10012
Phone: (646) 964-4383

#258
Kitchen Arts & Letters
Category: Bookstore
Average Price: Modest
Area: Upper East Side
Address: 1435 Lexington Ave
New York, NY 10128
Phone: (212) 876-5550

#259
Yunhong Chopsticks
Category: Kitchen & Bath
Average Price: Expensive
Area: Chinatown
Address: 50 Mott St
New York, NY 10013
Phone: (212) 566-8828

#260
Gateway Center
Category: Shopping Center,
Department Store
Average Price: Modest
Area: Spring Creek
Address: 409 Gateway Dr
Brooklyn, NY 11239
Phone: (718) 348-9477

#261
New Bo Bo Bicycle
Category: Bike Repair, Maintenance, Bikes
Average Price: Inexpensive
Area: Little Italy
Address: 96 Elizabeth St
New York, NY 10013
Phone: (212) 226-1668

#262
Goorin Bros.
Category: Accessories, Hats
Average Price: Expensive
Area: West Village
Address: 337 Bleecker Street
New York, NY 10014
Phone: (212) 256-1895

#263
4 Play Brooklyn
Category: Jewelry, Women's Clothing
Average Price: Modest
Area: South Slope, Park Slope
Address: 360 7th Ave
Brooklyn, NY 11215
Phone: (718) 369-4086

#264
Village Style
Category: Used, Vintage
Average Price: Modest
Area: East Village, Alphabet City
Address: 111 E 7th St
New York, NY 10009
Phone: (212) 260-6390

#265
So Good Jewelry
Category: Jewelry
Average Price: Inexpensive
Area: Soho
Address: 448 Bdwy
New York, NY 10013
Phone: (212) 625-9552

#266
Joe Fresh
Category: Women's Clothing, Men's Clothing
Average Price: Modest
Area: Flatiron
Address: 110 5th Ave
New York, NY 10011
Phone: (212) 366-0960

#267
Stewart/Stand Design Store
Category: Home Decor, Cards, Stationery
Average Price: Modest
Area: DUMBO
Address: 141-A Front St
Brooklyn, NY 11201
Phone: (718) 875-1204

#268
Century 21
Category: Department Store
Average Price: Modest
Area: Upper West Side
Address: 1972 Broadway
New York, NY 10023
Phone: (212) 518-2121

#269
Kate Spade
Category: Women's Clothing
Average Price: Expensive
Area: Upper East Side
Address: 789 Madison Ave
New York, NY 10065
Phone: (212) 988-0259

#270
Anthropologie
Category: Women's Clothing, Home Decor
Average Price: Expensive
Area: Union Square, Flatiron
Address: 85 5th Ave
New York, NY 10003
Phone: (212) 627-5885

#271
Desert Island
Category: Comic Books, Bookstore
Average Price: Modest
Area: Williamsburg - North Side
Address: 540 Metropolitan Ave
Brooklyn, NY 11211
Phone: (718) 388-5087

#272
Reiss
Category: Men's Clothing, Women's Clothing
Average Price: Expensive
Area: West Village
Address: 313 Bleecker St
New York, NY 10014
Phone: (212) 488-2411

#273
Trash & Vaudeville
Category: Men's Clothing,
Women's Clothing, Accessories
Average Price: Expensive
Area: East Village
Address: 4 St Marks Pl
New York, NY 10003
Phone: (212) 982-3590

#274
Jacks 99 Cent Store
Category: Discount Store
Average Price: Inexpensive
Area: Midtown East
Address: 16 E 40th St
New York, NY 10016
Phone: (212) 696-5767

#275
Verameat Jewelry
Category: Jewelry, Accessories
Average Price: Modest
Area: East Village
Address: 315 E 9th St
Manhattan, NY 10003
Phone: (212) 388-9045

#276
Sunday Brunch
Category: Women's Clothing
Average Price: Expensive
Area: Fort Greene
Address: 164 Lafayette Ave
Brooklyn, NY 11238
Phone: (646) 410-3455

#277
Apple Store
Category: Electronics, Computers
Average Price: Expensive
Area: Midtown East
Address: 767 5th Ave
New York, NY 10153
Phone: (212) 336-1440

#278
Lion In The Sun
Category: Cards, Stationery
Average Price: Modest
Area: Park Slope
Address: 232 7th Ave
Brooklyn, NY 11215
Phone: (718) 369-4006

#279
Goodwill Store
Category: Thrift Store
Average Price: Inexpensive
Area: Sunnyside
Address: 47-47 Van Dam St
Long Island City, NY 11101
Phone: (718) 392-0125

#280
Alexis Bittar
Category: Jewelry
Average Price: Expensive
Area: West Village
Address: 353 Bleecker St
New York, NY 10014
Phone: (212) 727-1093

#281
University Housewares
Category: Home Decor
Average Price: Expensive
Area: Morningside Heights
Address: 2901 Broadway
New York, NY 10025
Phone: (212) 882-2798

#282
Century 21
Category: Department Store
Average Price: Modest
Area: Lefrak City
Address: 61-01 Junction Blvd
Rego Park, NY 11374
Phone: (718) 699-2121

#283
Lion In The Sun
Category: Cards, Stationery
Average Price: Modest
Area: Park Slope
Address: 232 7th Ave
Brooklyn, NY 11215
Phone: (718) 369-4006

#284
The Sample Room NY
Category: Bridal
Average Price: Expensive
Area: Flatiron
Address: 40 W 17th St
New York, NY 10011
Phone: (212) 929-8868

#285
**Green Village Used Clothing
& Furniture**
Category: Thrift Store,
Discount Store, Used, Vintage
Average Price: Inexpensive
Area: Bushwick
Address: 276 Starr St
Brooklyn, NY 11237
Phone: (718) 599-4017

#286
Crossroads Trading Co
Category: Men's Clothing, Women's Clothing,
Used, Vintage
Average Price: Modest
Area: Williamsburg - North Side
Address: 135 N 7th St
Brooklyn, NY 11211
Phone: (718) 387-3010

#287
Buffalo Exchange
Category: Vintage, Women's Clothing,
Men's Clothing
Average Price: Modest
Area: Williamsburg - North Side
Address: 504 Driggs Ave
Brooklyn, NY 11211
Phone: (718) 384-6901

#288
Comptoir Des Cotonniers
Category: Women's Clothing,
Children's Clothing
Average Price: Expensive
Area: Soho
Address: 155 Spring St
New York, NY 10012
Phone: (212) 274-0830

#289
Rag & Bone
Category: Women's Clothing, Men's Clothing
Average Price: Expensive
Area: West Village
Address: 104 Christopher St
New York, NY 10014
Phone: (212) 727-2990

#290
Musu
Category: Gift Shop
Average Price: Modest
Area: East Village
Address: 305 E 9th St
New York, NY 10003
Phone: (212) 673-5057

#291
Bed Bath & Beyond
Category: Home Decor, Kitchen & Bath
Average Price: Modest
Area: Jackson Heights
Address: 72-15 25th Ave
East Elmhurst, NY 11369
Phone: (718) 429-9438

#292
Tierra
Category: Jewelry
Average Price: Modest
Area: Soho
Address: 65 Spring St
New York, NY 10012
Phone: (646) 476-5343

#293
Housing Works Thrift Shop
Category: Thrift Store, Used, Vintage
Average Price: Inexpensive
Area: Kips Bay, Gramercy
Address: 157 E 23rd St
New York, NY 10010
Phone: (212) 529-5955

#294
Target
Category: Department Store
Average Price: Modest
Area: Marine Park, Flatbush
Address: 1598 Flatbush Ave
Brooklyn, NY 11210
Phone: (718) 637-5005

#295
Louis Purple
Category: Men's Clothing,
Bespoke Clothing, Formal Wear
Average Price: Expensive
Area: Noho
Address: 323 Lafayette
New York, NY 10012
Phone: (212) 219-8559

#296
Angela's Vintage Boutique
Category: Used, Vintage, Women's Clothing
Average Price: Modest
Area: East Village
Address: 26 2nd Ave
New York, NY 10003
Phone: (212) 475-0101

#297
J.Crew
Category: Men's Clothing, Accessories,
Women's Clothing
Average Price: Expensive
Area: Tribeca
Address: 235-237 West Broadway
New York, NY 10013
Phone: (212) 226-5476

#298
Midtown Comics
Category: Comic Books, Toy Store
Average Price: Modest
Area: Midtown West, Theater District
Address: 200 W 40th St
New York City, NY 10018
Phone: (212) 302-8192

#299
Save On Fifth
Category: Discount Store, Women's Clothing
Average Price: Inexpensive
Area: Park Slope
Address: 421 5th Ave
Brooklyn, NY 11215
Phone: (718) 965-2040

#300
Save Khaki
Category: Men's Clothing
Average Price: Expensive
Area: Noho
Address: 317 Lafayette St
New York, NY 10012
Phone: (212) 925-0130

#301
H & M
Category: Women's Clothing,
Department Store
Average Price: Inexpensive
Area: Midtown West
Address: 1328 Broadway
New York, NY 10001
Phone: (646) 473-1165

#302
Greenlight Bookstore
Category: Bookstore
Average Price: Modest
Area: Fort Greene
Address: 686 Fulton St
Brooklyn, NY 11217
Phone: (718) 246-0200

#303
Dinosaur Hill
Category: Toy Store, Hobby Shop
Average Price: Modest
Area: East Village
Address: 306 E 9th St
New York, NY 10003
Phone: (212) 473-5850

#304
Kiki De Montparnasse
Category: Lingerie, Women's Clothing
Average Price: Exclusive
Area: Soho
Address: 79 Greene St
New York, NY 10012
Phone: (212) 965-8070

#305
Mr. Closeout
Category: Department Store, Outlet Store
Average Price: Inexpensive
Area: Financial District
Address: 145 Fulton St
New York, NY 10038
Phone: (212) 227-7775

#306
TJ Maxx
Category: Department Store
Average Price: Modest
Area: Manhattan Valley
Address: 808 Columbus Ave
New York, NY 10025
Phone: (212) 222-0543

#307
Rags-A-Gogo
Category: Used, Vintage
Average Price: Modest
Area: West Village
Address: 218 W 14th St
New York, NY 10011
Phone: (646) 486-4011

#308
Shown To Scale
Category: Men's Clothing, Women's Clothing
Average Price: Modest
Area: Greenpoint
Address: 67 W St
Brooklyn, NY 11222
Phone: (347) 987-4729

#309
Trunk
Category: Women's Clothing
Average Price: Expensive
Area: DUMBO
Address: 68 Jay St
New York, NY 11201
Phone: (718) 522-6488

#310
The Meat Market Brooklyn
Category: Used, Vintage, Bridal
Average Price: Inexpensive
Area: Bedford Stuyvesant
Address: 380 Tompkins Ave
Brooklyn, NY 11216
Phone: (347) 927-1238

#311
Kate Spade
Category: Leather Goods, Accessories
Average Price: Expensive
Area: Soho
Address: 454 Broome St
New York, NY 10013
Phone: (212) 274-1991

#312
Designers Promise
Category: Women's Clothing
Average Price: Modest
Area: Financial District
Address: 93 Nassau St
New York, NY 10038
Phone: (212) 513-1532

#313
Catbird
Category: Jewelry
Average Price: Expensive
Area: Williamsburg - North Side
Address: 219 Bedford Ave
Brooklyn, NY 11211
Phone: (718) 599-3457

#314
The Upper Rust Antiques
Category: Antiques
Average Price: Modest
Area: East Village, Alphabet City
Address: 445 E 9th St
New York, NY 10009
Phone: (212) 533-3953

#315
Teddy
Category: Women's Clothing, Accessories
Average Price: Modest
Area: Park Slope
Address: 202 5th Ave
Brooklyn, NY 11217
Phone: (718) 623-0500

#316
Shishi
Category: Women's Clothing
Average Price: Modest
Area: Upper West Side
Address: 2488 Broadway
New York, NY 10025
Phone: (646) 692-4510

#317
Topshop
Category: Women's Clothing, Accessories
Average Price: Expensive
Area: Soho
Address: 478 Broadway
New York, NY 10012
Phone: (212) 966-9555

#318
Exit 9 Gift Emporium
Category: Cards, Stationery,
Accessories, Toy Store
Average Price: Modest
Area: Cobble Hill, Boerum Hill
Address: 127 Smith St
Brooklyn, NY 11201
Phone: (718) 422-7720

#319
The Reed Space
Category: Accessories, Men's Clothing
Average Price: Expensive
Area: Lower East Side
Address: 151 Orchard St
New York, NY 10002
Phone: (212) 253-0588

#320
Marc Jacobs
Category: Men's Clothing,
Women's Clothing, Accessories
Average Price: Expensive
Area: Soho
Address: 163 Mercer St
New York, NY 10012
Phone: (212) 343-1490

#321
Shoegasm
Category: Shoe Store
Average Price: Modest
Area: West Village, Meatpacking District
Address: 71 8th Ave
New York, NY 10014
Phone: (212) 691-2091

#322
99 Cent Dreams
Category: Discount Store
Average Price: Inexpensive
Area: Midtown West
Address: 2 W 46th St
New York, NY 10036
Phone: (212) 840-1995

#323
Printed Matter
Category: Bookstore, Art Gallery
Average Price: Modest
Area: Chelsea
Address: 195 10th Ave
New York, NY 10011
Phone: (212) 925-0325

#324
Greenwich Letterpress
Category: Cards, Stationery
Average Price: Expensive
Area: West Village
Address: 39 Christopher St
New York, NY 10014
Phone: (212) 989-7464

#325
Brandy Melville
Category: Women's Clothing, Accessories
Average Price: Modest
Area: Soho
Address: 518 Broadway
New York, NY 10012
Phone: (646) 707-3119

#326
Reciprocal NYC
Category: Sporting Goods, Arcade
Average Price: Modest
Area: East Village
Address: 402 E 11th St
New York, NY 10009
Phone: (212) 388-9191

#327
Barney's New York
Category: Women's Clothing, Accessories
Average Price: Expensive
Area: Upper West Side
Address: 2151 Broadway
New York, NY 10023
Phone: (646) 335-0978

#328
Moulded Shoe Company
Category: Shoe Store
Average Price: Expensive
Area: Midtown East
Address: 10 E 39th St Lbby
New York, NY 10016
Phone: (212) 683-9389

#329
NBA Store
Category: Sports Wear
Average Price: Modest
Area: Midtown West
Address: 590 5th Ave
New York, NY 10036
Phone: (212) 515-6221

#330
Edith Machinist
Category: Women's Clothing, Used, Vintage
Average Price: Expensive
Area: Lower East Side
Address: 104 Rivington St
New York, NY 10002
Phone: (212) 979-9992

#331
Furnish Green
Category: Furniture Store,
Home Decor, Antiques
Average Price: Modest
Area: Midtown West, Koreatown
Address: 1261 Broadway
New York, NY 10001
Phone: (917) 583-9051

#332
Werk A.K.A. Gesamtkunstwerk
Category: Jewelry, Accessories
Average Price: Modest
Area: Lower East Side
Address: 9 Clinton St
Manhattan, NY 10002
Phone: (646) 476-9100

#333
Bencraft Hatters
Category: Accessories, Men's Clothing
Average Price: Modest
Area: Williamsburg - South Side,
South Williamsburg
Address: 236 Broadway
Brooklyn, NY 11211
Phone: (718) 384-5517

#334
Zara
Category: Men's Clothing, Women's Clothing
Average Price: Modest
Area: Soho
Address: 580 Broadway
New York, NY 10012
Phone: (212) 343-1725

#335
Urban Space Meatpacking
Category: Wholesale Store
Average Price: Modest
Area: West Village, Meatpacking District
Address: 829 Washington St
New York, NY 10014
Phone: (212) 633-0185

#336
Cook's Arts & Crafts
Category: Arts, Crafts
Average Price: Inexpensive
Area: Glendale
Address: 80-09 Myrtle Ave
Glendale, NY 11385
Phone: (718) 366-6085

#337
Urban Outfitters
Category: Women's Clothing, Men's Clothing
Average Price: Modest
Area: Financial District
Address: 182 Broadway
New York, NY 10038
Phone: (212) 962-0642

#338
New & Almost New
Category: Used, Vintage
Average Price: Modest
Area: Little Italy
Address: 171 Mott St
New York, NY 10012
Phone: (212) 226-6677

#339
Epaulet Shop
Category: Men's Clothing
Average Price: Expensive
Area: Lower East Side
Address: 144 Orchard St
New York, NY 10002
Phone: (212) 228-3626

#340
O.N.A
Category: Women's Clothing
Average Price: Modest
Area: Prospect Heights
Address: 593A Vanderbilt Ave
Brooklyn, NY 11238
Phone: (718) 783-0630

#341
Warby Parker HQ
Category: Eyewear, Opticians, Optometrists
Average Price: Modest
Area: South Village
Address: 161 Avenue Of The Americas
New York, NY 10012
Phone: (646) 517-5223

#342
A Uno Tribeca
Category: Women's Clothing
Average Price: Expensive
Area: Tribeca
Address: 123 W Broadway
New York, NY 10013
Phone: (212) 227-6233

#343
Brunello Cucinelli
Category: Men's Clothing, Women's Clothing
Average Price: Exclusive
Area: West Village
Address: 379 Bleecker St
New York, NY 10014
Phone: (212) 627-9202

#344
Meg
Category: Women's Clothing
Average Price: Expensivo
Area: Williamsburg - North Side
Address: 54 N 6th St
Brooklyn, NY 11211
Phone: (347) 294-0777

#345
Town & Village Hardware
Category: Hardware Store
Average Price: Modest
Area: Stuyvesant Town, Gramercy
Address: 337 1st Ave
New York, NY 10003
Phone: (212) 673-3192

#346
Grit N Glory
Category: Accessories, Men's Clothing,
Women's Clothing
Average Price: Modest
Area: Lower East Side
Address: 186 Orchard St
New York, NY 10002
Phone: (212) 253-2775

#347
Pinkyotto
Category: Women's Clothing
Average Price: Expensive
Area: Nolita
Address: 49 Prince St
New York, NY 10012
Phone: (212) 226-3580

#348
H&M
Category: Fashion
Average Price: Modest
Area: Flatiron
Address: 111 5th Ave
New York, NY 10003
Phone: (212) 539-1741

#349
Crate&Barrel
Category: Furniture Store, Department Store
Average Price: Modest
Area: Greenwich Village
Address: 611 Broadway
New York, NY 10012
Phone: (212) 780-0004

#350
Little King Jewelry
Category: Jewelry
Average Price: Modest
Area: Midtown West
Address: 37 W 47th St
New York, NY 10036
Phone: (212) 260-6140

#351
The Lego Store
Category: Toy Store
Average Price: Modest
Area: Midtown West
Address: 620 5th Ave
New York, NY 10020
Phone: (212) 245-5973

#352
Life Boutique Thrift
Category: Thrift Store, Used, Vintage
Average Price: Modest
Area: South Slope, Park Slope
Address: 515 5th Ave
Brooklyn, NY 11215
Phone: (718) 788-5433

#353
Buffalo Exchange
Category: Used, Vintage, Men's Clothing,
Women's Clothing
Average Price: Modest
Area: Cobble Hill
Address: 109 Boerum Pl
Brooklyn, NY 11201
Phone: (718) 403-0490

#354
Norman & Jules
Category: Toy Store
Average Price: Exclusive
Area: Park Slope
Address: 158 7th Ave
New York, NY 11215
Phone: (347) 987-3323

#355
West Elm Market
Category: Home Decor, Furniture Store,
Cards, Stationery
Average Price: Modest
Area: DUMBO
Address: 50 Washington St
Brooklyn, NY 11201
Phone: (718) 522-3498

#356
Rudy Volcano
Category: Accessories, Jewelry
Average Price: Modest
Area: Chelsea
Address: 167 Ave C 10th St
New York, NY 10009
Phone: (347) 969-4769

#357
Dig
Category: Nursery, Gardening
Average Price: Modest
Area: Boerum Hill
Address: 479 Atlantic Ave
Brooklyn, NY 11217
Phone: (718) 554-0207

#358
Journey
Category: Home Decor, Furniture Store
Average Price: Modest
Area: DUMBO
Address: 72 Front St
Brooklyn, NY 11201
Phone: (718) 797-9277

#359
Housing Works
Category: Thrift Store, Used, Vintage
Average Price: Inexpensive
Area: Soho
Address: 130 Crosby St
New York, NY 10012
Phone: (646) 786-1200

#360
Burberry
Category: Men's Clothing,
Women's Clothing, Accessories
Average Price: Expensive
Area: Soho
Address: 131 Spring Street
New York, NY 10012
Phone: (212) 925-9300

Apt 141
Category: Women's Clothing, Jewelry
Average Price: Expensive
Area: East Village
Address: 141 E 13th St
New York, NY 10003
Phone: (212) 982-4227

#362
3.1 Phillip Lim
Category: Women's Clothing,
Men's Clothing, Accessories
Average Price: Expensive
Area: Noho
Address: 48 Great Jones St
New York, NY 10012
Phone: (212) 334-1160

#363
Hamlet's Vintage
Category: Used, Vintage, Antiques
Average Price: Modest
Area: Greenwich Village
Address: 146 W 4th St
New York, NY 10012
Phone: (212) 228-1561

#364
Vinnie's Styles
Category: Women's Clothing, Men's Clothing
Average Price: Expensive
Area: Park Slope, Prospect Heights,
Boerum Hill
Address: 160 Flatbush Ave
Brooklyn, NY 11217
Phone: (718) 636-9787

#365
Hermès
Category: Women's Clothing,
Leather Goods, Accessories
Average Price: Exclusive
Area: Financial District
Address: 15 Broad St
New York, NY 10005
Phone: (212) 785-3030

#366
Lot Less Closeouts
Category: Department Store
Average Price: Inexpensive
Area: Chinatown, Civic Center
Address: 299 Broadway
New York, NY 10184
Phone: (212) 233-2146

#367
Rain Africa
Category: Skin Care, Cosmetics,
Beauty Supply
Average Price: Modest
Area: Midtown West
Address: 59 W 49th Street
New York, NY 10112
Phone: (212) 239-3070

#368
Urban Outfitters
Category: Fashion
Average Price: Modest
Area: Midtown West
Address: 1333 Broadway
New York, NY 10018
Phone: (212) 239-1673

#369
Longboard Loft
Category: Outdoor Gear
Average Price: Modest
Area: Lower East Side
Address: 132 Allen St
Manhattan, NY 10002
Phone: (212) 673-7947

#370
Jussara Lee
Category: Fashion
Average Price: Exclusive
Area: West Village
Address: 60 Bedford St
New York, NY 10014
Phone: (212) 242-4128

#371
Housing Works Thrift Shop
Category: Thrift Store
Average Price: Modest
Area: Hell's Kitchen, Midtown West,
Theater District
Address: 730 9th Ave
New York, NY 10019
Phone: (646) 963-2665

#372
New York Running Company
Category: Sports Wear, Shoe Store
Average Price: Modest
Area: Upper East Side
Address: 1051 3rd Ave
New York, NY 10065
Phone: (212) 223-8109

#373
Skingraft
Category: Men's Clothing, Leather Goods,
Women's Clothing
Average Price: Expensive
Area: Nolita
Address: 7 Prince St
New York, NY 10012
Phone: (212) 226-8467

#374
The Shape Of Lies
Category: Jewelry
Average Price: Modest
Area: East Village, Alphabet City
Address: 127 E 7th St
New York, NY 10009
Phone: (212) 533-5920

#375
Odin - East Village
Category: Men's Clothing
Average Price: Expensive
Area: East Village
Address: 328 E 11th St
New York, NY 10003
Phone: (212) 475-0666

#376
Dah Shop
Category: Bikes
Average Price: Inexpensive
Area: Chinatown, Lower East Side
Address: 134 Division St
New York, NY 10002
Phone: (212) 925-0155

#377
Zarin Fabrics
Category: Fabric Store, Shades & Blinds,
Furniture Store
Average Price: Expensive
Area: Lower East Side
Address: 69 Orchard Street
New York, NY 10002
Phone: (212) 925-6112

#378
Steven Alan
Category: Men's Clothing, Women's Clothing
Average Price: Expensive
Area: Tribeca
Address: 103 Franklin St
New York, NY 10013
Phone: (212) 343-0692

#379
Pony Shop
Category: Used, Vintage, Women's Clothing
Average Price: Modest
Area: Park Slope
Address: 69 5th Ave
New York, NY 11217
Phone: (718) 622-7669

#380
Ugly Luggage
Category: Antiques
Average Price: Modest
Area: Williamsburg - North Side
Address: 214 Bedford Ave
Brooklyn, NY 11211
Phone: (718) 384-0724

#381
Something Else On Fifth
Category: Women's Clothing, Men's Clothing
Average Price: Modest
Area: Park Slope
Address: 208 5th Ave
Brooklyn, NY 11215
Phone: (718) 230-4063

#382
H&M
Category: Children's Clothing,
Men's Clothing, Women's Clothing
Average Price: Modest
Area: Downtown Brooklyn
Address: 497-501 Fulton St
Brooklyn, NY 11201
Phone: (855) 466-7467

#383
Gansevoort Market
Category: Specialty Food,
Shopping, Food Court
Average Price: Modest
Area: West Village
Address: 52 Gansevoort St
New York, NY 10014
Phone: (212) 242-1701

#384
Turntable Lab
Category: Vinyl Records,
High Fidelity Audio Equipment
Average Price: Modest
Area: East Village, Alphabet City
Address: 120 E 7th St
New York, NY 10009
Phone: (212) 677-0675

#385
Brooklyn Industries
Category: Men's Clothing, Women's Clothing
Average Price: Expensive
Area: DUMBO
Address: 70 Front St
Brooklyn, NY 11201
Phone: (718) 797-4240

#386
Shinola
Category: Watches, Leather Goods, Bikes
Average Price: Expensive
Area: Tribeca
Address: 177 Franklin St.
New York, NY 10013
Phone: (917) 728-3000

#387
Bookcourt
Category: Bookstore
Average Price: Modest
Area: Cobble Hill
Address: 163 Court St
Brooklyn, NY 11201
Phone: (718) 875-3677

#388
Two Lovers Boutique
Category: Women's Clothing, Used, Vintage
Average Price: Modest
Area: Park Slope
Address: 227 5th Ave
Brooklyn, NY 11215
Phone: (718) 783-5683

#389
Forever 21
Category: Accessories, Women's Clothing
Average Price: Inexpensive
Area: Greenwich Village, Union Square
Address: 40 E 14th St
New York, NY 10003
Phone: (212) 228-0598

#390
Zakka
Category: Toy Store, Books,
Mags, Music, Video
Average Price: Modest
Area: DUMBO
Address: 155 Plymouth St
Brooklyn, NY 11201
Phone: (718) 801-8037

#391
Brooklyn Vaper
Category: Vape Shop
Average Price: Modest
Area: Williamsburg - North Side
Address: 240 Kent Ave
Brooklyn, NY 11249
Phone: (347) 871-7718

#392
Piperlime
Category: Women's Clothing
Average Price: Expensive
Area: Soho
Address: 121 Wooster St
New York, NY 10012
Phone: (212) 343-4284

#393
Fresh
Category: Cosmetics, Beauty Supply
Average Price: Expensive
Area: Union Square, Flatiron
Address: 872 Broadway
New York, NY 10003
Phone: (212) 477-1100

#394
J.J. Hat Center
Category: Hats
Average Price: Expensive
Area: Midtown West, Koreatown
Address: 310 5th Ave
New York, NY 10001
Phone: (212) 239-4368

#395
The Bargain Stop
Category: Department Store, Discount Store
Average Price: Inexpensive
Area: Astoria
Address: 3302 30th Ave
Astoria, NY 11103
Phone: (718) 777-0797

#396
Juice Pedaler
Category: Café, Bikes, Juice Bar
Average Price: Inexpensive
Area: Windsor Terrace
Address: 154 Prospect Park SW
Brooklyn, NY 11218
Phone: (718) 871-7500

#397
Book-Off
Category: Bookstore, Comic Books, Music, Dvds
Average Price: Inexpensive
Area: Midtown West
Address: 49 W 45th St
New York, NY 10036
Phone: (212) 685-1410

#398
Lancelotti Housewares
Category: Home Decor
Average Price: Modest
Area: East Village, Alphabet City
Address: 66 Ave A
New York, NY 10009
Phone: (212) 475-6851

#399
American Eagle Outfitters
Category: Women's Clothing, Men's Clothing, Accessories
Average Price: Modest
Area: Midtown West, Theater District
Address: 1551-1555 Broadway
Manhattan, NY 10036
Phone: (212) 205-7260

#400
Tokio 7
Category: Used, Vintage
Average Price: Expensive
Area: East Village
Address: 83 E 7th St
New York, NY 10003
Phone: (212) 353-8443

#401
Saja Boutlque
Category: Bridal
Average Price: Modest
Area: Nolita
Address: 250 Elizabeth St
New York, NY 10012
Phone: (212) 226-7570

#402
Papél New York
Category: Cards, Stationery
Average Price: Modest
Area: Cobble Hill
Address: 225 Court St
Brooklyn, NY 11201
Phone: (718) 422-0255

#403
Volang Boutique
Category: Jewelry, Women's Clothing
Average Price: Modest
Area: Lower East Side
Address: 147 Orchard St
Manhattan, NY 10002
Phone: (212) 529-3212

#404
Pookie & Sebastian
Category: Women's Clothing
Average Price: Expensive
Area: Midtown East, Murray Hill
Address: 541 3rd Ave
New York, NY 10016
Phone: (212) 951-7110

#405
Domus Unaffected Living
Category: Home Decor, Jewelry, Cards, Stationery
Average Price: Modest
Area: Hell's Kitchen, Midtown West
Address: 413 W 44th St
New York, NY 10036
Phone: (212) 581-8099

#406
Très Chix NYC
Category: Jewelry, Accessories
Average Price: Modest
Area: Hell's Kitchen, Midtown West
Address: 447 W 50th St
New York, NY 10019
Phone: (917) 592-9600

#407
H & M
Category: Men's Clothing, Women's Clothing, Department Store
Average Price: Modest
Area: Chelsea, Midtown West
Address: 435 7th Ave
New York, NY 10001
Phone: (212) 643-6955

#408
The Face Shop
Category: Cosmetics, Beauty Supply, Skin Care
Average Price: Modest
Area: Chinatown
Address: 6-B Elizabeth St
New York, NY 10013
Phone: (212) 608-1988

#409
Club Monaco
Category: Shopping
Average Price: Expensive
Area: Upper West Side
Address: 211 Columbus Avenue
New York, NY 10023
Phone: (212) 724-4076

#410
Club Monaco
Category: Shopping
Average Price: Expensive
Area: Upper West Side
Address: 211 Columbus Avenue
New York, NY 10023
Phone: (212) 724-4076

#411
Necessary Clothing
Category: Women's Clothing, Accessories
Average Price: Inexpensive
Area: Soho
Address: 442 Broadway
New York, NY 10013
Phone: (646) 214-7881

#412
Loom
Category: Cards, Stationery,
Home Decor, Jewelry
Average Price: Expensive
Area: Park Slope
Address: 115 7th Ave
Brooklyn, NY 11215
Phone: (718) 789-0061

#413
The Jewelry Patch
Category: Jewelry
Average Price: Modest
Area: Midtown West
Address: 501 Fashion Ave
New York, NY 10018
Phone: (212) 840-8279

#414
Extraordinary
Category: Home Decor, Gift Shop
Average Price: Modest
Area: Midtown East
Address: 247 E 57th St
New York, NY 10022
Phone: (212) 223-9151

#415
Goodwill
Category: Thrift Store
Average Price: Inexpensive
Area: Yorkville, Upper East Side
Address: 1704 2nd Ave
New York, NY 10128
Phone: (212) 831-1830

#416
Deals
Category: Discount Store
Average Price: Inexpensive
Area: Sunnyside
Address: 3909 Queens Blvd
Sunnyside, NY 11104
Phone: (718) 383-1391

#417
Some Odd Rubies
Category: Used, Vintage
Average Price: Expensive
Area: Lower East Side
Address: 151 Ludlow St
New York, NY 10002
Phone: (212) 353-1736

#418
A&G Merch
Category: Home Decor, Furniture Store
Average Price: Expensive
Area: Williamsburg - North Side
Address: 111 N 6th St
Brooklyn, NY 11249
Phone: (718) 388-1779

#419
Sephora
Category: Cosmetics, Beauty Supply
Average Price: Modest
Area: Union Square, Flatiron
Address: 45 E 17th St
New York, NY 10003
Phone: (212) 995-8833

#420
Brooklyn Vintage Bicycles
Category: Bikes
Average Price: Modest
Area: Gerritson Beach
Address: 51 Fane Ct
Brooklyn, NY 11229
Phone: (347) 733-2079

#421
The Frye Company
Category: Fashion
Average Price: Expensive
Area: Soho
Address: 113 Spring St
New York, NY 10012
Phone: (212) 226-3793

#422
Ad Hoc
Category: Men's Clothing, Leather Goods, Women's Clothing
Average Price: Expensive
Area: Williamsburg - North Side
Address: 135 Wythe Ave
Brooklyn, NY 11211
Phone: (718) 302-2462

#423
Chanel
Category: Women's Clothing
Average Price: Exclusive
Area: Upper East Side
Address: 737 Madison Ave
New York, NY 10021
Phone: (212) 535-5505

#424
The Great Frog
Category: Jewelry
Average Price: Expensive
Area: Lower East Side
Address: 72 Orchard St
Manhattan, NY 10002
Phone: (646) 370-5727

#425
Alter
Category: Women's Clothing
Average Price: Modest
Area: Greenpoint
Address: 140 Franklin St
Brooklyn, NY 11222
Phone: (718) 349-0203

#426
ENZ's
Category: Women's Clothing
Average Price: Modest
Area: East Village
Address: 125 2nd Ave
New York, NY 10003
Phone: (917) 841-5989

#427
Cosmetic Market
Category: Cosmetics, Beauty Supply
Average Price: Inexpensive
Area: Midtown East
Address: 15 E 37th St
New York, NY 10016
Phone: (212) 725-3625

#428
The Shoe Tree
Category: Shoe Store
Average Price: Modest
Area: Morningside Heights
Address: 2876 Broadway
New York, NY 10025
Phone: (212) 280-1711

#429
Pageant Print Shop
Category: Antiques, Bookstore
Average Price: Modest
Area: East Village
Address: 69 4th St E
New York, NY 10003
Phone: (212) 674-5296

#430
Thrift & New Shop
Category: Used, Vintage
Average Price: Modest
Area: Hell's Kitchen, Midtown West, Theater District
Address: 602 9th Ave
New York, NY 10036
Phone: (212) 265-3087

#431
Sephora
Category: Cosmetics, Beauty Supply
Average Price: Expensive
Area: Midtown West, Theater District
Address: 1500 Broadway
New York, NY 10036
Phone: (212) 944-6789

#432
Rime
Category: Men's Clothing, Shoe Store
Average Price: Modest
Area: Cobble Hill, Boerum Hill
Address: 157 Smith St
Brooklyn, NY 11201
Phone: (718) 797-0675

#433
Blue Tree
Category: Women's Clothing, Children's
Clothing, Accessories
Average Price: Exclusive
Area: Upper East Side
Address: 1283 Madison Ave
New York, NY 10128
Phone: (212) 369-2583

#434
Prada Broadway
Category: Shoe Store, Leather Goods
Average Price: Exclusive
Area: Soho
Address: 575 Broadway
New York, NY 10012
Phone: (212) 334-8888

#435
Patagonia
Category: Sports Wear, Outdoor Gear, Hats
Average Price: Expensive
Area: Upper West Side
Address: 426 Columbus Ave
New York, NY 10024
Phone: (917) 441-0011

#436
PS Fabrics
Category: Fabric Store
Average Price: Inexpensive
Area: Chinatown
Address: 359 Broadway
New York, NY 10013
Phone: (212) 226-1534

#437
Worship
Category: Used, Vintage, Women's Clothing
Average Price: Modest
Area: Bushwick
Address: 117 Wilson Ave
Brooklyn, NY 11237
Phone: (718) 484-3660

#438
Kill Devil Hill
Category: Customized Merchandise
Average Price: Modest
Area: Greenpoint
Address: 170 Franklin St
Brooklyn, NY 11222
Phone: (347) 534-3088

#439
Toys R Us
Category: Toy Store
Average Price: Modest
Area: Midtown West, Theater District
Address: 1514 Broadway
New York, NY 10036
Phone: (646) 366-8800

#440
David Owens Vintage Clothing
Category: Used, Vintage
Average Price: Expensive
Area: Lower East Side
Address: 154 Orchard Street
New York, NY 10002
Phone: (212) 677-3301

#441
Chrysanthemum
Rare Teas & Flowers
Category: Florist, Tea Room, Chocolate Shop
Average Price: Modest
Area: Crown Heights, Prospect Heights
Address: 669 Washington Ave
New York, NY 11238
Phone: (347) 955-5401

#442
Dave's Wear House
Category: Sports Wear, Bikes
Average Price: Inexpensive
Area: Little Italy, Chinatown
Address: 123 Baxter St
Manhattan, NY 10013
Phone: (212) 334-1958

#443
Buffalo Exchange
Category: Used, Vintage, Men's Clothing,
Women's Clothing
Average Price: Inexpensive
Area: East Village
Address: 332 E 11th St
New York, NY 10003
Phone: (212) 260-9340

#444
Paragon Sports
Category: Outdoor Gear,
Sports Wear, Shoe Store
Average Price: Expensive
Area: Union Square, Flatiron
Address: 867 Broadway
New York, NY 10003
Phone: (212) 255-8889

#445
Heaven Street
Category: Vinyl Records
Average Price: Modest
Area: East Williamsburg, Bushwick
Address: 184 Noll St
Brooklyn, NY 11237
Phone: (718) 381-5703

#446
Lululemon Athletica
Category: Sports Wear, Women's Clothing
Average Price: Expensive
Area: Union Square, Flatiron
Address: 15 Union Sq W
New York, NY 10003
Phone: (212) 675-5286

#447
Brooklyn Industries
Category: Accessories, Men's Clothing,
Women's Clothing
Average Price: Modest
Area: Greenwich Village
Address: 801 Broadway
New York, NY 10003
Phone: (646) 478-8871

#448
Artist & Craftsman Supply
Category: Art Supplies
Average Price: Modest
Area: Sunnyside
Address: 34-09 Queens Blvd
Long Island City, NY 11101
Phone: (718) 433-4949

#449
Puro Chile
Category: Home Decor, Ethnic Food
Average Price: Modest
Area: Chinatown
Address: 221 Ctr St
New York, NY 10013
Phone: (212) 925-7876

#450
Gap Outlet
Category: Men's Clothing, Women's Clothing,
Children's Clothing
Average Price: Modest
Area: Downtown Brooklyn
Address: 400 Fulton St
Brooklyn, NY 11201
Phone: (718) 855-8574

#451
Good Records NYC
Category: Music, Dvds
Average Price: Modest
Area: East Village
Address: 218 E 5th St
New York, NY 10003
Phone: (212) 529-2081

#452
Habit
Category: Women's Clothing
Average Price: Modest
Area: Park Slope
Address: 137 5th Ave
New York, NY 11217
Phone: (718) 399-7467

#453
India Sari Palace
Category: Women's Clothing
Average Price: Modest
Area: Jackson Heights
Address: 3707 74th St
Jackson Heights, NY 11372
Phone: (718) 426-2700

#454
Madewell
Category: Women's Clothing, Accessories
Average Price: Expensive
Area: Flatiron
Address: 115 5th Ave
New York, NY 10003
Phone: (212) 228-5172

#455
Sterling Place
Category: Home Decor,
Antiques, Furniture Store
Average Price: Expensive
Area: South Slope, Park Slope
Address: 352 7th Ave
Brooklyn, NY 11215
Phone: (718) 499-4800

#456
Pier 1 Imports
Category: Home Decor
Average Price: Modest
Area: Upper East Side
Address: 1110 3rd Ave
New York, NY 10065
Phone: (646) 358-1360

#457
Rabbits
Category: Women's Clothing, Used, Vintage
Average Price: Expensive
Area: Williamsburg - South Side
Address: 120 Havemeyer St
Brooklyn, NY 11211
Phone: (718) 384-2181

#458
Gap
Category: Children's Clothing,
Men's Clothing, Women's Clothing
Average Price: Modest
Area: Midtown West
Address: 680 5th Ave
New York, NY 10019
Phone: (212) 977-7023

#459
Housing Works
Category: Used, Vintage
Average Price: Modest
Area: Brooklyn Heights
Address: 122 Montague St
Brooklyn, NY 11201
Phone: (718) 237-0521

#460
Meg Cohen Design Shop
Category: Accessories
Average Price: Modest
Area: South Village
Address: 59 Thompson St
New York, NY 10012
Phone: (212) 966-3733

#461
Ted's Fine Clothing
Category: Men's Clothing
Average Price: Modest
Area: Lower East Side
Address: 155 Orchard St
New York, NY 10002
Phone: (212) 966-2029

#462
Sterling Place
Category: Home Decor, Antiques,
Furniture Store
Average Price: Expensive
Area: South Slope, Park Slope
Address: 352 7th Ave
Brooklyn, NY 11215
Phone: (718) 499-4800

#463
C. Wonder
Category: Home Decor,
Women's Clothing, Accessories
Average Price: Modest
Area: Soho
Address: 72 Spring St
New York, NY 10012
Phone: (212) 219-3500

#464
Headhoods
Category: Women's Clothing, Men's Clothing
Average Price: Modest
Area: Williamsburg - North Side
Address: 86 Berry St
Brooklyn, NY 11211
Phone: (917) 620-5327

#465
Urban Outfitters
Category: Men's Clothing, Women's Clothing
Average Price: Modest
Area: Yorkville, Upper East Side
Address: 1511 3rd Ave
New York, NY 10028
Phone: (212) 288-0275

#466
DQM New York
Category: Sporting Goods, Shoe Store
Average Price: Modest
Area: East Village
Address: 7 E 3rd St
New York, NY 10003
Phone: (212) 505-7551

#467
Aritzia
Category: Women's Clothing
Average Price: Expensive
Area: Soho
Address: 524 Broadway
New York, NY 10012
Phone: (212) 965-2188

#468
Shine 32
Category: Jewelry
Average Price: Modest
Area: Midtown West, Koreatown
Address: 35 W 32nd St
New York, NY 10001
Phone: (212) 564-4004

The Face Shop
Category: Skin Care, Cosmetics, Beauty Supply
Average Price: Modest
Area: Midtown West, Koreatown
Address: 35 W 32nd St
New York, NY 10001
Phone: (212) 967-0515

#470
Village Party Store
Category: Costumes, Party Supplies
Average Price: Inexpensive
Area: Greenwich Village
Address: 13 E 8th St
New York, NY 10003
Phone: (212) 675-9697

#471
Telco Discount Stores
Category: Discount Store
Average Price: Inexpensive
Area: Bensonhurst
Address: 6708 18th Ave
Brooklyn, NY 11204
Phone: (718) 621-2120

#472
We The People
Category: Women's Clothing
Average Price: Expensive
Area: Lower East Side
Address: 156 Stanton St
Manhattan, NY 10002
Phone: (212) 533-1091

#473
Niketown
Category: Sporting Goods, Shoe Store
Average Price: Expensive
Area: Midtown East
Address: 6 E 57th St
New York, NY 10022
Phone: (212) 891-6453

#474
Neda
Category: Women's Clothing
Average Price: Expensive
Area: Cobble Hill, Carroll Gardens
Address: 302 Court St
Brooklyn, NY 11231
Phone: (718) 624-6332

#475
Exstaza Limited
Category: Women's Clothing
Average Price: Inexpensive
Area: Soho
Address: 491 Broadway
New York, NY 10012
Phone: (212) 925-8193

#476
Church Street Surplus
Category: Used, Vintage
Average Price: Expensive
Area: Tribeca
Address: 327 Church St
New York, NY 10013
Phone: (212) 226-5280

#477
3x1
Category: Men's Clothing, Women's Clothing
Average Price: Exclusive
Area: Soho, Tribeca
Address: 15 Mercer St
Manhattan, NY 10013
Phone: (212) 391-6969

#478
Amazing Savings
Category: Discount Store
Average Price: Inexpensive
Area: Midwood
Address: 1415 Ave M
Brooklyn, NY 11230
Phone: (718) 998-2020

#479
Worth & Worth
Category: Accessories, Hats
Average Price: Modest
Area: Midtown West
Address: 45 W 57th St
New York, NY 10019
Phone: (212) 265-2887

#480
Metropolis
Category: Used, Vintage, Thrift Store
Average Price: Expensive
Area: East Village
Address: 43 3rd Ave
New York, NY 10003
Phone: (212) 358-0795

#481
Unique Boutique Donation Center
Category: Used, Vintage
Average Price: Inexpensive
Area: Upper West Side
Address: 487 Columbus Ave
New York, NY 10024
Phone: (212) 362-8877

#482
The Bag Man
Category: Shopping
Average Price: Inexpensive
Area: Midtown West
Address: 261 West 34th Street
New York, NY 10001
Phone: (212) 502-5452

#483
Cog & Pearl
Category: Home Decor, Jewelry
Average Price: Expensive
Area: Park Slope
Address: 190 5th Ave
Brooklyn, NY 11217
Phone: (718) 623-8200

#484
Beauty 35
Category: Cosmetics, Beauty Supply
Average Price: Inexpensive
Area: Hell's Kitchen, Midtown West
Address: 505 8th Ave
New York, NY 10018
Phone: (212) 563-1010

#485
Otto
Category: Accessories,
Women's Clothing, Lingerie
Average Price: Modest
Area: South Slope, Park Slope
Address: 354 7th Ave
Brooklyn, NY 11215
Phone: (718) 788-6627

#486
Ted Baker London
Category: Men's Clothing, Women's Clothing
Average Price: Expensive
Area: Soho
Address: 107 Grand St
New York, NY 10013
Phone: (212) 343-8989

#487
Brand Hunters
Category: Thrift Store, Women's Clothing
Average Price: Inexpensive
Area: Bedford Stuyvesant, Bushwick
Address: 1083 Broadway
New York, NY 11221
Phone: (718) 455-5372

#488
Dor L' Dor
Category: Women's Clothing
Average Price: Modest
Area: Financial District
Address: 80 Nassau St
New York, NY 10038
Phone: (212) 227-4949

#489
Argosy Book Store
Category: Antiques, Art Gallery, Bookstore
Average Price: Expensive
Area: Midtown East
Address: 116 E 59th St
New York, NY 10022
Phone: (212) 753-4455

#490
Opening Ceremony
Category: Men's Clothing, Women's Clothing
Average Price: Expensive
Area: Soho
Address: 35 Howard St
New York, NY 10013
Phone: (212) 219-2688

#491
Park Delicatessen
Category: Florist, Men's Clothing
Average Price: Modest
Area: Crown Heights
Address: 722 Classon Ave
Brooklyn, NY 11238
Phone: (718) 789-8889

#492
Chanel
Category: Men's Clothing, Women's Clothing
Average Price: Exclusive
Area: Soho
Address: 139 Spring St Frnt
New York, NY 10012
Phone: (212) 334-0055

#493
PIQ
Category: Home Decor,
Hobby Shop, Gift Shop
Average Price: Modest
Area: Midtown West
Address: 74 W 50th St
New York, NY 10112
Phone: (212) 227-9273

#494
Shareen
Category: Bridal
Average Price: Modest
Area: Flatiron
Address: 13 W 17th St
New York, NY 10011
Phone: (212) 206-1644

#495
**Michael's - The Consignment
Shop For Women**
Category: Women's Clothing,
Used, Vintage, Shoe Store
Average Price: Expensive
Area: Upper East Side
Address: 1041 Madison Ave
New York, NY 10075
Phone: (212) 737-7273

#496
A Lovely Universe
Category: Women's Clothing, Jewelry
Average Price: Modest
Area: Boerum Hill
Address: 103 Bond St
Brooklyn, NY 11217
Phone: (718) 596-4135

#497
Hanger
Category: Women's Clothing
Average Price: Modest
Area: Astoria
Address: 30-74 Steinway St
Astoria, NY 11103
Phone: (347) 808-9093

#498
Guenevere Rodriguez
Category: Jewelry
Average Price: Modest
Area: Williamsburg - South Side
Address: 309 Bedford Ave
Brooklyn, NY 11211
Phone: (718) 387-4878

#499
Extra Butter LES
Category: Sports Wear, Shoe Store, Hats
Average Price: Modest
Area: Lower East Side
Address: 125 Orchard St
New York, NY 10002
Phone: (917) 965-2500

#500
Museum Of Modern Art Design Store
Category: Art Gallery, Jewelry
Average Price: Modest
Area: Midtown West
Address: 44 W 53rd St
New York, NY 10019
Phone: (212) 767-1050

Made in the USA
Middletown, DE
17 September 2022